Read and Play

Farm Animals

by Jim Pipe

Aladdin/Watts
London • Sydney

farm

2

Here is a **farm**.

What lives on a **farm**?

3

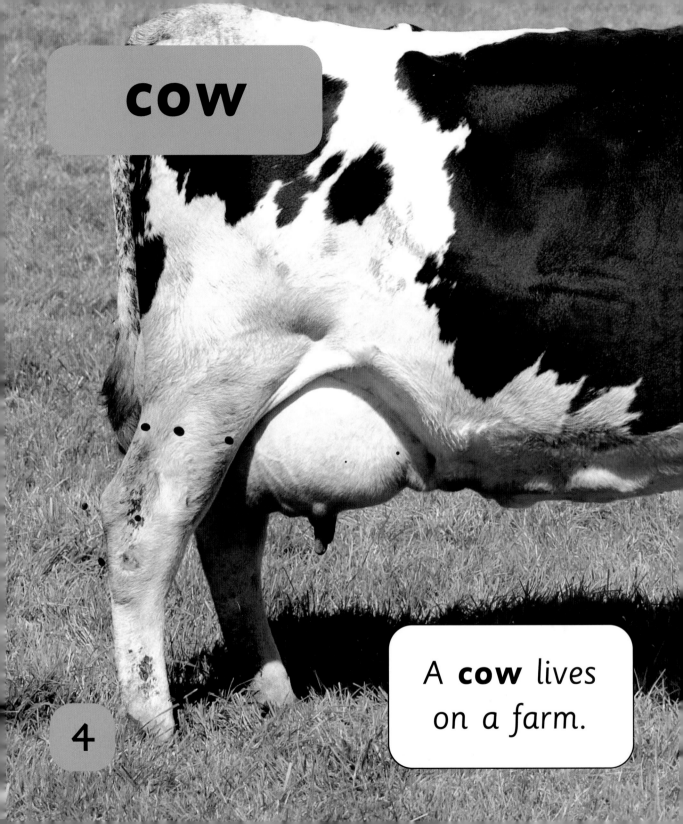

COW

A **cow** lives on a farm.

4

A **cow** eats grass.

5

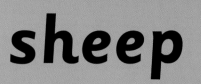

sheep

6

Sheep live on a farm.

This is a flock of **sheep**.

pig

8

Pigs live on a farm.

A **pig**
loves mud!

9

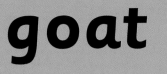
goat

Goats live on a farm.

A billy **goat** has horns.

chicken

A **chicken** lives on a farm.

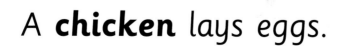

A **chicken** lays eggs.

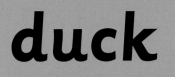

duck

Ducks live on a farm.

turkey

A **turkey** lives on a farm.

15

donkey

16

Donkeys live on a farm.

A **donkey** has big ears!

horse

Horses help a farmer.

Dogs help a farmer too.

Who am I?

donkey

turkey

goat

sheep

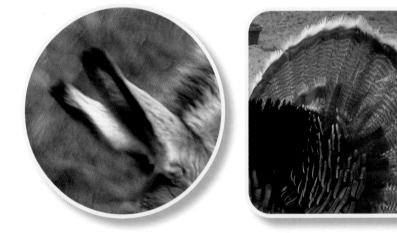

20 Match the words and pictures.

How many?

Can you count the chickens?

21

What noise?

Moo!

Hee-haw!

Quack!

Oink!

22 Make a sound like these animals!

Index

Can you find these pictures of farm animals in the book?

For Parents and Teachers

Questions you could ask:

p. 2 What lives on a farm? As well as farm animals, you could also mention wild animals such as foxes, rabbits, mice, rats and owls.

p. 5 What drink do we get from a cow? Milk. You could point out cow's udders on picture.

p. 6 What do we get from a sheep? e.g. wool. The farmer shears the sheep (this doesn't hurt sheep). Wool is used to make jumpers, socks, coats etc.

p. 9 Why do you think pigs like mud? They roll in mud to keep themselves cool. They love to root under the ground using their snout to look for food.

p. 11 A billy goat is a father goat. What other animal fathers do you know? Bull, cockerel, ram etc.

p. 12 What is a chicken covered in? Feathers. You could point out body parts, e.g. beak, comb, eyes.

p. 14 Do ducks like water? Yes, they are good swimmers and look for food under the water.

p. 16 What does a donkey's coat feel like? Soft and hairy. Compare with other farm animals.

p. 19 How can dogs help a farmer? They round up/herd animals such as cows and sheep.

p. 20 If they need a clue, children can look back to pages 6, 11, 15 and 16.

Activities you could do:

• Introduce farm animals by singing "Old Macdonald Had a Farm", "Baa Baa Black Sheep", "Goosey Goosey Gander", "Little Bo Peep", "Mary Had a Little Lamb" and other rhymes and songs.

• Role play: ask the reader to act out their favourite farm animal, e.g. strutting like a chicken, sniffing like a pig, chewing like a cow, adding noises! Or they could be a farmer looking after animals.

• Play sorting and counting games with plastic farm animals. Introduce group names, e.g. flock.

• Talk about animal babies on a farm, such as kids (see page 10), piglets, lambs, chicks and calves.

• Create a farm display using a variety of collage materials to make farm animals.

Paperback Edition 2009
© Aladdin Books Ltd 2006

Designed and produced by
Aladdin Books Ltd
PO Box 53987
London SW15 2SF

First published in 2006
by Franklin Watts
338 Euston Road
London NW1 3BH

Franklin Watts Australia
Level 17/207 Kent Street
Sydney NSW 2000

Franklin Watts is a division of Hachette Children's Books, an Hachette Livre UK company.
www.hachettelivre.co.uk

ISBN 978 0 7496 8972 8

A catalogue record for this book is available from the British Library.

Dewey Classification: 636

Printed in Malaysia
All rights reserved

Series consultant
Zoe Stillwell is an experienced Early Years teacher currently teaching at Pewley Down Infant School, Guildford.

Photocredits:
l-left, r-right, b-bottom, t-top, c-centre, m-middle
All photos from istockphoto.com except: 2-3, 23tl — Corbis.
18-19, 23bl — Corel.